D1322554

Working for Myself

WITHDRAWN

WITHDRAWN

CRAFTING A BUSINESS

Tana Reiff

AGS®

American Guidance Service, Inc.
Circle Pines, Minnesota 55014-1796
1-800-328-2560

Working for Myself

Beauty and the Business
Clean as a Whistle
Cooking for a Crowd
The Flower Man
The Green Team
Handy All Around
Other People's Pets
You Call, We Haul
Your Kids and Mine

Cover Illustration: James Balkovek
Cover Design: Ina McInnis
Text Designer: Diann Abbott

Printed in the United States of America
ISBN 0-7854-1109-7 (Previously ISBN 1-56103-904-7)
Product Number 40832
A 0 9 8 7 6 5 4 3 2

C O N T E N T S

Chapter

CHAPTER 1

Gifts from the Forest

It was late afternoon in the forest. A chilly breeze made the leaves dance. Night time was not far off.

Greg kicked at a small pile of leaves. "Look at that, Andrea," he said to his girlfriend. "Brown and yellow leaves already! Fall is on its way."

"It's been a good summer," Andrea said as she looked up at him.

"And this has been a nice little

camping trip," Greg added.

"It has," Andrea said. "I sure will hate to go back to work tomorrow."

"Me, too."

The leaves crunched under their feet as they walked back to their camp.

Just then, Greg bent down. "Look at that!" he said. He picked up a twig and held it out to Andrea. "Only Mother Nature could come up with a shape as beautiful as this."

Greg put the twig into his backpack, along with the other twigs, stones, and feathers he had found. He threw the backpack over his shoulder again. It was getting heavy.

"We should go," Andrea said.

"What a great red feather!" said Greg, as if he hadn't heard her. He plucked a tiny feather from a bush and put it in his backpack.

As they walked on, Greg's head began to fill with pictures. He was imagining all the things he would make when he got home. On his workshop bench, the twigs, stones, and feathers would become jewelry. To make earrings, he would bend the twigs into interesting shapes and add feathers. To make necklaces and bracelets, he would braid the longer twigs. To finish them, he would add stones and feathers.

"You have a wonderful eye, Greg. You can see things in twigs, stones, and feathers that other people don't see," Andrea said with a warm smile.

"Thanks, honey," Greg said. "I guess I do." As he said that, he spotted a rock and picked it up. "Look at this! It's a rock shaped like a turtle."

"A *turtle*?" Andrea asked. "I don't see a turtle."

"Look!" Greg pointed. "There's the head. There's the shell. And there's the tail peeking out."

Andrea could only laugh. Yet she wished she could see what Greg saw.

"OK, let's get going," said Greg. Now

he couldn't wait to get home and paint the turtle rock.

In a few minutes they reached their camp. They got the tent down just before dark. As quickly as they could, they packed up everything and hiked back to Greg's car.

On the trail along the way, Greg spotted a large knot of very old wood lying on the ground.

"Look at that!" he said. "I can make some great pins out of that!"

"Pins?" Andrea asked. "It's just a piece of old wood. What made you think of pins?"

"It's a *great* piece of wood," Greg told her. "It's from one of those big lumps on a tree trunk. If you cut it real thin, you can see all the little circles in it. Just wait until I show you!"

He picked up the piece of wood and stuffed it into his backpack.

"How much farther is it to the car?" Greg asked Andrea. "It's getting dark."

"We're almost there," Andrea said.

That was just like Greg. He was always looking at the sights along the way. He was always thinking of how something ordinary could be turned into something special. It was Andrea who always found the way to where they were going.

The next morning Greg and Andrea returned to the working world. Greg was back at the telephone company. Andrea was back at the gift shop.

Right after work, though, Greg was down in his basement. He used a tiny brush to paint the turtle rock. He painted the head and eyes in great detail. Tiny stroke by tiny stroke, he painted a perfect turtle shell. He painted four feet and a tail. He made the rock look almost like a real turtle.

The next night, Greg worked only on earrings. He cut, sanded, and shaped wood. He carved wooden beads. He combined bits of wood and feathers into new forms. He glued the pieces together and then added ear wires.

The night after that, Greg worked on necklaces and bracelets. He had soaked the longer twigs for a few days. Now he could bend them into circles. He added beads, stones, and feathers.

On the fourth night, he made pins. After cutting the wood into thin slices, he cut the slices into different shapes. Then he lightly sanded each piece and brushed on a finish. Finally he glued a pin back to each.

At the end of the week, Greg laid out everything he had made. He had five pairs of earrings, three necklaces, two bracelets, and ten pins. He had turned gifts from the forest into gifts for people. Greg had been very busy. It only occurred to him now that he hadn't seen Andrea all week.

CHAPTER 2

Crafts for Sale

On Friday afternoon Andrea called Greg at work. "Where have you been all week?" she asked.

"I'm sorry," said Greg. "I guess the time just got away from me."

"I know it did. I called you a few times," Andrea said. "But every time your father said that you were working down in the basement. I told him not to bother you."

"I'm sorry," Greg said.

"How about if I come over later?" Andrea asked.

"Sure," said Greg. "I want you to see what I've made."

Andrea was at Greg's place right after dinner. His father let her in, and she headed for the basement. Greg was at his workbench, waiting for her.

"Why are your hands behind your back?" Andrea said, laughing.

Greg brought his hands around in front of him. "For you," he said. In his hands was a pin he'd made. He pushed Andrea's long hair out of the way and pinned it to her jacket.

Andrea looked down at it. "Oh, it's beautiful," she said.

"I hope it makes up for not seeing you all week," Greg said.

"Well . . ." Andrea said. Then she smiled. "I guess so."

Greg couldn't wait to show Andrea everything he had made. She picked up each piece. "These are really very good,

Greg," she said. "Your ideas are so fresh, and everything is so well made. Now what are you going to do with this stuff? It's a crime to keep selling things for next to nothing at your mother's garage sales. You're not being fair to yourself."

"I've told you. These things I make are like a part of me." Greg looked a little embarrassed. "I guess I feel nervous about showing them off in the real world."

"But these things are your *work*—not you," Andrea said.

"My work and I are . . . well, kind of one and the same," said Greg. "I mean, that's how I feel about it."

"Oh, you really *are* an artist inside, aren't you," said Andrea. "I love it."

Greg smiled. "I may work at a plain old job at the phone company," he said. "But inside I do feel like an artist."

"Listen, Greg. Do you remember Mrs. Lane, the owner of the gift shop? She really wants to see your stuff," said

Andrea. "Can I take a few of your things with me to show her?"

Greg ran his long, thin fingers through his light hair. He looked as if he had seen a ghost. Then at last he said, "All right. You can show Mrs. Lane a few things."

He picked out what he felt were his best pieces. One pair of earrings. One bracelet. One necklace. One pin.

"How about the turtle rock?" Andrea asked. "I think it's great."

"No, not the turtle rock," said Greg quietly. "I'm not ready to show anyone the turtle rock."

The next day Andrea carried a flat box into the gift shop. She felt excited as she lifted the lid to show Mrs. Lane what was inside.

"I've been waiting a long time to see these things," said Mrs. Lane. "You talk so much about them." She put her hands to her mouth as the lid came off the box. "They're lovely!" she gasped.

"Do you think we could sell them

here?" Andrea asked her.

"I'd like to," said Mrs. Lane. "But your friend must understand how the business works. I take crafts only on consignment. Do you understand what consignment is?"

"Yes," said Andrea. "It means that the store owner doesn't *buy* the crafts. The store just *sells* them for the craftsperson. Then when something sells, the store gets part of the money."

"That's right," said Mrs. Lane. She handed Andrea a form. "You take this to Greg. Tell him to look it over. If he agrees, he can list each piece of jewelry he wants to put in my shop. Have him sign the bottom of the form.

"The system is easy. As I sell each piece, I'll mark it off right on the form. At the end of each month, I'll pay Greg. He gets 70 percent of the sales price. I keep 30 percent."

Andrea gave Greg the form that evening. "Mrs. Lane takes 30 percent, huh? And then I have to wait for the money? Why can't I just sell the jewelry to her?" Greg said.

"Most stores that carry crafts only sell on consignment," Andrea said. "It seems like a fair system. And you'd still make more than you would from a yard sale," she pointed out.

"True," Greg said.

Together Andrea and Greg worked out prices for the different kinds of jewelry. The basic materials cost nothing. As Greg often said, they were gifts from nature. Andrea wrote down how much Greg paid for paint, wood finish, glue, earring wires, and pin backs. She asked him to guess how long it took him to make each piece. Then she asked him about his overhead.

"Overhead?" he said.

"You know, your rent, telephone bills, stamps—what it costs to sell things. Stuff like that."

"I don't pay rent on this basement,"

Greg said. "And I don't even have a telephone line to pay for."

"Well, fine. Low overhead keeps your prices low," Andrea said. "OK. Let's figure it out. What's the cost of materials plus the cost of labor plus overhead?" She used that figure as a basis to come up with prices for all of Greg's things. "What do you think?" she asked him.

"I'd be really happy to get 70 percent of those prices," said Greg.

"We'll just give Mrs. Lane a few things at a time," said Andrea.

"Right," said Greg. "Let's see how they sell."

"Oh, I know that people will love them," Andrea said.

She was right. Greg's crafts were a big hit at the gift shop. Mrs. Lane soon asked for more. Greg's first check came at the end of the month.

"Wow! People must really like me," Greg told Andrea. He seemed very surprised by his success.

"I don't know about *you*," she said with a laugh. "But they sure do like your jewelry!"

CHAPTER 3

Making a Business

"Your crafts sell so well at Mrs. Lane's gift shop," Andrea said one day. "You could sell things at other places, too."

"Would Mrs. Lane mind if I placed my jewelry in other shops?" Greg wondered aloud.

"The form you signed says that you can sell at other shops. Just not within 20 miles of Mrs. Lane's."

Greg was ready to try other shops. The

following Saturday he and Andrea visited five gift shops in nearby towns. They took along a nice variety of Greg's new pieces.

They worked out deals with three shops that day. The shops in Steelville and Newburg took some jewelry on consignment. The shop in Bell City was willing to pay for things up front.

"What a great day!" said Greg on the drive home. "Let's stop for dinner!"

"OK," said Andrea. "But, Greg, *I'd* better drive. You're all over the road!"

"I'm just so happy! Imagine! My work is going to be on display in four shops! I just can't believe it!"

"It's wonderful," Andrea said. "But let me drive, OK?"

Greg pulled over, and Andrea took the wheel. Greg got in the car from the other side. He was so excited he could hardly sit still.

"Relax!" Andrea told him.

They ate at a little diner along the

road. It wasn't anything fancy. But to Greg, the paper napkins were fine linen and the plastic cups were crystal. His spirits were as high as a kite.

"I promised these shop owners a lot more stuff," Greg said. "When am I ever going to have time to make it all?"

"Let's just see how it goes for now," Andrea said. She patted his arm.

"Could you help me?" Greg asked. "I can design the jewelry. How about if you help put it together? It's not hard. I'll teach you."

"OK," said Andrea. "I'm glad to help. In return, you can take me out to dinner now and then."

"OK," Greg promised.

But three months went by before they had time to go out to dinner.

They were happy to be spending a lot of time together. Night after night the two of them worked in Greg's basement. On weekends they took walks in the woods to find more materials. It was a busy time, but a good time for both of them.

Mrs. Lane's shop kept selling more of his things. Greg got a check every month, right on time.

Still, not everything was going smoothly. The shop in Steelville sent only one check in three months, and it was late. "We're going to have to drop that shop," Andrea said.

So that Saturday she and Greg went to Steelville to get Greg's things. The shop was closed. The sign on the door said *Out of Business*.

"Great," said Greg. "It looks like I'm out a lot of money."

Andrea spent the following Monday morning on the phone. She tried to track down the owner of the Steelville shop. She found that a lot of other people were looking for the same man. The best she could do was to get her name on a list. Everyone on the list wanted something from the shop, either merchandise or money. Everyone was angry.

The Newburg shop was also a problem, but for a different reason. It was selling Greg's things, but not many. When Greg and Andrea visited that shop, they saw what the problem was.

Some of Greg's crafts had been placed in the front window. The sun had beat down on them until the wood cracked. No one would buy jewelry in that condition.

Inside the shop, Greg's things were hard to find. They had been placed in back of some big, shiny brass jewelry.

Andrea spoke with the shop owner. "These natural materials can't take the hot sun in the front window," she explained. "And no one can see these beautiful pieces the way you display them back there."

The owner moved Greg's jewelry to the top shelf of the glass case. Andrea took the cracked pieces of jewelry out of the front window. She didn't leave any new ones in their place.

With a better display, more of Greg's things began to sell at the Newburg shop.

The arrangement with the Bell City shop needed work, too. From her experience at the gift shop, Andrea knew what to do. She worked out a new price list. The shop could buy Greg's things wholesale. That meant they would get 50 percent off the list prices. Andrea made an order form, too. From now on the shop would pay for shipping. That would save a lot of driving around.

Andrea kept records of every piece of Greg's work that went out. She kept records of every penny that came in. She also found two more stores to sell things to at wholesale.

Three months after that first drive to the shops, Greg and Andrea went out to dinner again. Over a wonderful meal, Greg pulled out a tiny velvet box from his pocket.

"I have something for you," he began.

"This one, I did not make."

Andrea opened the box. Inside was a beautiful ring. The stone glowed in the soft light.

"We've already become partners in the craft business," Greg said. "I'd like us to be partners in life. I love you, Andrea. Will you marry me?"

"Yes," Andrea said, smiling. She leaned across the table and kissed him.

C H A P T E R   4

Show Time

Greg and Andrea were married in the spring. After their honeymoon they moved into an apartment of their own. Greg continued to work at the phone company, Andrea at the gift shop. They kept one small room in their apartment for craftwork.

One day early in the summer, they had caught up with their craft work. They didn't need to go looking for materials.

They didn't need to visit any shops that weekend.

Andrea had an idea. "Let's go to the craft show over at the fairgrounds. I'd like to take a good look at what other people are selling."

"Good idea!" Greg said.

Even though Greg loved to make things, he'd never seen a craft show. He couldn't believe his eyes. "Look at this! Look at that!" he kept saying.

People walked by row upon row of craft booths. They stopped to look at things, touch things, and lay out their money. There were wooden toys, silver jewelry, and glass sun catchers. There were hand-made brooms, clay pots, and brightly painted chairs. There was something for almost everyone.

"I would love to show my work like this!" Greg said. "I wonder how you get into this kind of a show."

Andrea spotted a small sign: *Show Manager*. Inside a red striped tent, a woman stood behind a table. "My name is Mimi," she said. "May I help you?"

"We were wondering how my husband could get his work into a craft show like this," Andrea said.

"What is it that you make?" the woman asked Greg.

Greg told the woman all about his nature crafts.

"Your work sounds interesting," said Mimi. "Do you have slides?"

"*Slides?* Do you mean pictures?" Andrea asked.

"Yes. We ask to see slides before we talk about show contracts." Mimi explained that this was a "juried" show. A group of judges looked at all the slides. They invited only the top craft artists to be in the show.

"Not all shows are juried," Mimi went on. "Some of the shows will let in any craftsperson who pays. That can be a good way to start. But I think you'll find juried shows your best bet."

"I see," said Andrea.

"I'd be happy to look at your slides," said Mimi with a big smile.

"We'll have to take some pictures first," said Greg.

"Why don't you pay someone to do it for you?" Mimi suggested. "Remember, we look at *hundreds* of slides. Some of the pictures aren't very good. We look a little closer at the better pictures."

"Where do the booths come from?" Andrea asked.

"You bring your own. Some people buy one that's already built. Or you can build it yourself. It can be a wooden stand or a tent. Whatever works best for what you are selling."

Greg and Andrea were both a bit surprised at how much went into a craft show. They thanked Mimi, then looked around the show some more. They talked as they walked.

"You can get full retail price at a show," said Andrea. "That's more than you can get from consignment or by wholesaling. That is, if your pieces sell well. You still have to pay rent for your booth and other expenses."

"I want to do a show," Greg said.

"Well, let's work on it," Andrea said.

Over the next few weeks, they got a photographer to take pictures of Greg's work. The woman set up each piece of jewelry in front of a white cloth backdrop. She made each and every piece look perfect.

Andrea sent the slides to Mimi. Getting into a juried show would now be a matter of waiting.

Andrea also sent for a list of all the upcoming craft shows in the area. Greg signed up for some that were not juried. Booth rent was low for these shows. Greg thought they would be good practice for a juried show.

A month later Greg and Andrea got ready for the first show. They built a booth. They made the back wall of the booth in five main pieces. Each tall piece was a wooden frame. Thick cloth was stretched over the inside of each frame and stapled to the back. Jewelry could be pinned to the cloth. The pieces fit together to make a U-shaped wall. Each piece had two legs that fit on the bottom. All the pieces came apart and folded on hinges. That way they fit snugly in the car trunk.

On the front of the booth, Greg put two ladders. Then he laid three boards across the two ladders to make shelves. That's where painted rocks and other crafts would be placed.

They packed two large umbrellas to fit over the booth if it rained. They packed two folding chairs and a steel box for money. They bought a pad of sales slips at an office supply store. They made sure to take bags, boxes, and tissue paper, too.

Andrea also sent for a tax number from the state. They would have to add sales tax to every sale. Later, they would have to send that extra money to the state.

By the time the show date came, Greg and Andrea were tired.

"I wish we could quit our day jobs," Greg said. "We're putting a lot of time into this business."

"You said it," Andrea said. "Maybe someday this will be our only job."

CHAPTER 5

Horses and Crafts

It took nearly an hour to pack the car for that first craft show. First Greg and Andrea laid the shelf boards in the trunk. Then they put in the large and small pieces of their booth. They tied the ladders to the car roof. They laid the boxes of crafts in the back seat.

"Andrea, the door won't close!" Greg called from his side.

Andrea came around the car. She

poked her head inside and moved some boxes around. Then she pushed the door closed. "There," she said. "Snug as a bug in a rug."

Greg laughed. "OK, we're off," he said. "Now, where are we going?"

The show was at a big park only 20 miles away. Greg had never been there. Andrea had been there only once or twice with her parents. But she knew the way. Still, it took 40 minutes to get there because Greg drove so slowly.

"I don't want anything to break," he kept saying.

"What can break?" Andrea said. "This car's packed so tight, nothing can move!"

They laughed and talked all the way there. "I'm so excited," said Greg.

When they got to the park, there were horses everywhere. People were walking horses, riding horses, grooming horses. "I thought this was a craft show *and* a horse show," Andrea said. "All that I see around here is horses."

They drove around the park. In a few minutes they found the craft show. The manager took Greg and Andrea to their booth space.

There were only 12 spaces. Greg and Andrea set up their booth. They pinned the jewelry to the cloth back. They put the larger things on the ladder shelves. Greg set the turtle rock right in the middle. It was the first time he had ever put it out.

Everything was ready in plenty of time. Greg and Andrea even had time to look around before the show opened.

"Look at that!" Greg pointed across the way. The booth facing them had some nice wooden toys on display.

"Yes, and look at that one!" Andrea said. She pointed to a booth full of paintings. "That's *art*? Those pictures look really *ugly* to me," she whispered in Greg's ear.

"And look at that guy over there!" Greg whispered back. "He's selling key chains that were made in a factory!"

"I don't know about this show," Andrea said. "Maybe coming here was a mistake."

The show opening came and went. There was no rush of people, no crowd. A few people walked through. No one bought anything. It was clear that most of the people had come to the park for the horse show.

As the day went on, more people drifted over from the horse show. Greg and Andrea sold a few pieces of jewelry. No one even looked at the turtle rock. By noon Greg wrapped it up and put it in a box.

Finally he said, "I get the feeling that this craft show doesn't go with the horse show."

"Me, too," said Andrea. "Maybe the other shows will be better. I hope we get into that juried one."

Andrea filled out only ten sales slips the whole day. She added up all the money. It didn't even cover what they had paid to rent the booth space.

"Bad news," she told Greg. "We lost money on this one."

Greg couldn't help but feel a little let down. But he only said, "I know that my stuff is better than what we saw today."

"It sure is, Greg," said Andrea. "It's *much* better."

During the next few months, Greg and Andrea did five more shows. The first indoor show went better than the horse show. Greg and Andrea didn't make any money—but at least they broke even.

For the next outdoor show, Greg decided to make lots of little feather pins. They sold for only a few dollars each. And a lot of them sold. Those little pins alone paid the booth rent.

A show at a fire hall was a bust. People came to eat a ham dinner, not to buy crafts. Even the little feather pins didn't help. Greg and Andrea lost money.

The Good Neighbors show was a fundraiser. Most of the money earned would help people who were having a hard time. Greg and Andrea didn't make much that weekend. But they were glad to help the Good Neighbors.

During that show, Greg joined a crafts workers' co-op. Now he could go in with other craft artists to buy glue, paint, and other materials. That would cut down his overhead.

The show at the college turned out to be the best yet. It was held during the fall. People came to shop for holiday gifts. Greg and Andrea sold dozens of pairs of earrings. They sold necklace-and-bracelet sets in gift boxes. They sold most of everything they had.

Still, there was no word on the juried show. They tried to be patient. Andrea checked the mail every day.

At last a letter came with Mimi's return address on it. Andrea tore open the envelope. "We are very sorry to tell you . . ." the letter began. Inside it said that hundreds of applications had come in for just thirty empty spaces.

Andrea didn't know how to tell Greg the bad news. She made sure she read him the end of the letter. It said, "Please try again next time." They'd just have to wait a little while longer to get into a juried show.

CHAPTER 6

Party Plan

Greg was upset by the news about the juried show. "I guess I'm not as good as you thought," he said.

"Your work is *very* good," Andrea told him. "We'll keep trying to get into a juried show. Maybe you can come up with some new ideas. Then we'll make new slides and send them in."

"I didn't tell you yet, but I already have a new idea," said Greg.

The new idea was a headband. He made the band itself out of bent wood. Then he put feathers on it.

Andrea tried it on. "It sure is *different*," she said.

"You look great!" said Greg.

"I like it," said Andrea. "I really do. I think you have a winner here."

"I was thinking about making wreaths, too," Greg went on. "You know, with dried flowers and leaves and nice things we find in the woods. I think we could do well on wreaths."

"And *I* have a new idea, too," said Andrea. "It's a different way to sell."

"Tell me more."

"Well, you know how some people have parties in their homes to sell stuff? Like kitchen things or toys? Well, we could have parties to sell crafts. We could print a catalog with pictures of your work. We could take orders and make just the pieces that people want."

"Interesting. But our place is so small.

How could we have parties here?"

"We could give the parties in other people's homes," Andrea explained. "The people who hold the parties would get a cut of everything we sell."

"And I would have to go out and show the stuff?"

"You or me. We could both do it. What do you think?"

"I guess we could try it," said Greg.

"Let's start out with only jewelry," Andrea said.

Greg thought that was a good idea. After all, something like a turtle rock was a one-of-a-kind item.

So Andrea worked up a small catalog of Greg's work. She had the slides made into pictures. She wrote a few lines about each piece of jewelry. She tried to describe everything in just the most interesting way. Then she had the catalog printed.

Andrea's mother said she'd be more than happy to hold the first party. She invited her closest friends. She laid out cookies and punch and greeted everyone as they came in.

Greg and Andrea both went to the party. "I can't quite see these older women wearing my jewelry," Greg whispered to Andrea.

"Just remember that they have daughters and daughters-in-law," Andrea whispered back.

Greg and Andrea showed samples of the jewelry.

"How interesting," said one woman. But she spoke as if she didn't mean it.

"Where did you come up with these ideas?" asked another woman.

Greg and Andrea looked at each other. They remembered laughing at other people's art. They were both thinking that this party may have been a big mistake.

Then one woman said, "I know my daughter-in-law would *love* these feather earrings. She and her friends like to see who can find the most interesting earrings!"

Andrea's mother passed out catalogs and pencils. The women looked through the catalogs. Then, one by one, they began filling out their order forms. They handed Andrea their orders as they said good-bye.

Andrea started adding up the orders. Greg walked around the house. He couldn't sit down.

"You won't believe this," Andrea said at last. "We got enough orders tonight to keep us busy for the next two weeks!"

Greg looked at the numbers. "Are you sure you added right?" he asked.

"Add it up yourself!" Andrea told him. Then she turned to her mother. "You'll be seeing Greg's jewelry on a lot of your friends' kids!"

Andrea's mother was excited, too. "I have a lot more friends," she said. "Some of them are younger, too, you know," she added laughing. "I'll throw more parties."

"Don't forget that *you'll* make some money out of it, too!" Greg said.

"Oh, I don't want any money," said Andrea's mother. "I'm just happy to help you get your business going."

After that night Andrea worked all the parties. Greg stayed home and made jewelry. The parties took the place of some of the craft shows.

Then Greg and Andrea had a real surprise. They found out they had a baby on the way! That news made them very happy—but also worried. "How are we going to run this craft business with a child around?" Greg said. "It's hard enough as it is."

"We'll work it out," Andrea said.

"We can't both work full-time *and* have a baby *and* make crafts *and* do shows and parties," Greg said. "It's just too much. *Way* too much. There's only one answer. You'll have to quit your job at the gift shop."

"That might just work," said Andrea.

"The numbers on the crafts business are looking really good these days. If we budget very carefully, maybe we can get by on your paycheck plus the business."

"I think so," Greg said.

So just before the baby came, Andrea quit her job. Greg didn't stop worrying. But after the baby was born, he felt better when he saw how Andrea ran her days. While the baby slept, she was on the phone. Or she put jewelry together. She got something done every minute of the day.

And then, when baby Emma was only four months old, an important letter came. It was from Mimi. Greg had been accepted for his very first juried show.

CHAPTER 7

Good Show

The juried show felt different. Like the other shows, it had crafts, crafts, and more crafts. The craftspersons came in all shapes and sizes, all ages, all types. But this show was better. Greg felt it. Andrea saw it.

The show was laid out along a path around a lake. Ducks and geese swam there, putting on their own show behind the circle of craft booths. Huge green trees shaded the booths and walkways from the day's hot sun.

Andrea's favorite booth was full of glass. There were glass bowls. Glass vases. Glass everything. Light from behind shone through every piece. The morning sun seemed to bounce from one side of the booth to the other and back again. Holding the baby in her arms, Andrea watched in delight.

Greg had never seen wooden crafts as nice as those on display. There were mirrors set in fine carved wood. There were fine wooden chairs polished as smooth as silk. There were boxes made to show off the wood's beautiful grain.

"I can't believe that I got into this show!" Greg said to Andrea.

"You would not have been accepted if your work wasn't good enough," Andrea said. "Your crafts are works of art! You just have to start believing in yourself. That's all!"

"I don't know," said Greg. "I think I

may be lucky to sell anything at all here."

"Let's just wait and see," Andrea told him. "I think you'll be surprised."

Everything was ready. The booth was set up. Jewelry, headbands, and wreaths hung on the back frame in neat rows. Painted rocks were placed along the shelves. The turtle rock, which still had not sold, sat right in the middle. A tiny price tag hung from each piece.

The money box was under a small table in the front. It was tucked out of sight next to the bags, boxes, and tissue paper they'd bought. Sales slips and business cards were set out on top of the table.

Just before the show opened, Mimi stopped by. "I'll take the rest of your booth rent now," she said. Andrea wrote out a check. Then Mimi said, "This show offers prizes, you know. Would you like to enter a piece for the judges' panel to review?"

"I don't know," said Greg.

"You have nothing to lose," said Mimi

with a warm smile.

"All right," said Greg. "Take that necklace over there. You can show that to the judges."

Andrea laid the necklace in a nice box and Mimi took it with her.

"This makes me nervous," Greg said. "Now we'll see for sure that my stuff really doesn't belong in a fancy show like this one."

Andrea laid baby Emma in her basket. She was asleep when the show opened. Crowds of people filled the path around the lake.

Greg sat a little table at the back of the booth. He was making pins to show people how he worked. Andrea stood out front greeting everyone who walked by. She knew Greg's crafts inside out, so she could answer any questions.

Greg looked up and saw Andrea writing the first sales slip. "Thank you very much," he heard her say.

He watched out of the corner of his eye

as Andrea sold earrings, necklaces, and bracelets. He watched her sell two painted rocks and three wreaths. The booth was starting to look empty.

"We have a few more wreaths in the car," Andrea said. "Why don't you go and get them?"

Greg was glad to leave the booth for a while. The short walk to the car and back took 20 minutes.

Andrea was in the middle of selling a painted rock when Emma woke up. She had no choice but to hold the baby while she talked to people. When Greg came back, she handed the baby to him. He seemed very happy to leave the customers to her.

Three hours into the show, Andrea was getting hungry. "Greg, would you please go pick up some food?" she called out to the back of the booth.

She didn't see that Greg was talking to someone. This time he wasn't in such a hurry to get away from the booth,

Andrea noticed.

By the middle of the afternoon, Greg was just as busy as Andrea. Both of them showed people the crafts. Both of them made sales.

"We're doing great," Andrea said. "But I can't believe we still haven't sold the turtle rock. It's the best piece of all! What's wrong with people?"

Minutes later a woman came into the booth and picked up the turtle rock. She turned it over and over. "This is the most beautiful thing I have ever seen," she said. "I'll take it."

All of a sudden Greg said, "Oh, no! It's not for sale!"

Andrea's mouth dropped open. She looked at her husband, but she didn't say anything. The woman holding the turtle rock turned to Andrea.

"I'm sorry. The artist says it's not for sale," Andrea said.

The woman left the booth in a huff.

"Sorry," said Greg after she was gone.

"I just couldn't part with it after all. Maybe we could keep it for Emma."

Andrea just smiled. She wrapped the turtle rock in tissue paper. Then she put it in a box and tucked it under the table.

C H A P T E R   8

In the News

The crafts the judges had reviewed were set up in a small building by the lake. Mimi had said that the winners would be posted at 2 P.M. on the second day of the show.

"I'm going over to see the winners," Andrea told Greg.

"And leave me in the booth alone?"

"You'll do fine," Andrea said. She took the baby along. What she saw was a show within a show. On display were the very best crafts from each booth. Beautiful works of glass, wood, clay, paint, cloth, and metal were lined up on the walls and shelves.

The prize for Best of Show went to an iron cooking spoon. The beautiful hand-crafted piece sat in the center of the room on a stand by itself. A blue ribbon hung beside it.

The other winners were on the walls and shelves. Each one wore a ribbon. Andrea walked along slowly, admiring all the crafts.

Greg's necklace hung right under a light. Andrea had never seen his work look more beautiful. Then she spotted the blue ribbon next to it. It said *Best by a New Craftsperson*.

Maybe the ribbon goes with the wool cape on the other side, Andrea thought to herself. But no, the cape had its own ribbon: *Best Weaving*. Andrea had to catch her breath. There was no mistake!

Greg's necklace had won a blue ribbon!

Andrea couldn't move. This was Greg's first juried show, and he had won a prize! Then she saw the man with the camera. He was from the local newspaper.

"Is this yours?" he asked Andrea, pointing to Greg's necklace.

"No, it's my husband's."

"Is he here? I'd like to take a picture of him with his work."

"Will you wait?" Andrea asked. "I can get him in a minute."

She held onto Emma and ran down the path to get Greg.

"You won! You won!" she screamed as she reached the booth.

"Won what? Are there door prizes?" Greg said, laughing.

"You won the prize for Best by a New Craftsperson! A man from the paper wants to take your picture!"

"Don't joke about that," Greg said. "It's not funny."

"I'm not joking!" Andrea shouted.

"Hurry over there. I'll watch the booth. You go get your picture taken!"

The ribbon also came with a nice check. Greg smiled as his picture was taken. He smiled again when a woman came up and wrote him another check to buy the necklace.

The next morning a picture of Greg and his winning necklace was in the newspaper. "Making Jewelry from Nature" read the photo caption.

Then the phone started ringing off the wall. Some of the calls were from wholesalers. One call was from the manager of a trade show just for gift shops. Many of the calls were from friends who had seen Greg's picture in the paper.

"This is wonderful!" cried Andrea.

"It is. It is," Greg said. "But we can't do a trade show. How would we ever make enough stuff to fill all the orders? I'm still working at the phone company five full days a week."

"We have to find a way," said Andrea. "How about this? You design the jewelry—just like you're doing now. But I won't be the only one to put it all together. Let's say that we gather up big boxes of twigs and stones and feathers. Then we'll pay people who are good with their hands to assemble the jewelry."

"What about the wreaths?"

"Same goes for the wreaths," said Andrea. "I know this can work."

Greg was willing to try Andrea's plan. It was an important new step for the business. But first they would have to find some skillful craft workers. Those people would have to be paid. And their work would have to be just right.

"I'd rather quit my job and do this full time," said Greg.

"I know you would, but can you hold on a little longer?" Andrea asked him. "I know this wasn't part of our plan—but we're expecting another baby. We still need that paycheck, Greg. And we *really* need your company health plan."

Greg was tired of fitting his crafts work into evenings and weekends. He didn't have enough time to spend with Emma. And he had no time at all for anything extra. Still, he knew that Andrea was right. Especially with the new baby coming.

For the time being, the prize-winning craftsperson would spend his days at the phone company. Greg longed to work at his craft all day, every day. Maybe next year, he thought. Maybe next year.

CHAPTER 9

Sorting Out

By the time baby Devin was born, Greg's craft work was bringing in good money. He had his work in ten gift shops now. Greg and Andrea were consigning his crafts to some shops, wholesaling to others. They were still giving the home parties. Greg was still entering the shows, some juried, some not. They had five people working for them out of their own homes. Without them they would never have been able to keep up with orders. And they still belonged to the buying co-op. Every month the co-op was saving them money on materials.

Greg and Andrea felt like circus jugglers, though. They were always trying to keep all the eggs of their business in the air. If one egg dropped, it would break. Then the whole "act" could be in trouble.

Greg was still working full time at the phone company. At home, he and Andrea and the two children were packed into their tiny apartment like fish in a can. Everyone had to sleep in the same room. There were piles of toys and craft supplies stacked up in every corner.

They couldn't give up the craft room. It wasn't very large. But they needed what little work space they had. Greg's favorite time was while he was working in there. He would step in, close the door, and shut out the rest of the world. He'd open the window wide because he didn't want the glue smell to hurt the children. Then he'd get to work—and think.

"I should be happy with how well things are going," he was thinking one evening. "I should be glad that my work is selling well. I'm so lucky to have a great wife and two beautiful children. I should thank my lucky stars that I have a steady job and extra money coming in besides. So, why don't I feel good about all this?" Greg asked himself.

He thought and thought, late into the night. He never heard the children go to bed. He lost all track of time.

At last he got up and left the craft room. He made his way to the bedroom in the dark. Andrea was sound asleep.

He shook her. "Andrea. Wake up!" Greg said. "We need to talk."

Andrea made a soft little moaning sound and rolled over on her side.

"Come on! We really need to talk!" Greg said again.

"Oh, Greg, not now! Can't it wait until

tomorrow morning?" Andrea begged.

"No, it can't!" said Greg. "We have a three-ring circus going on here. I can't stand it anymore! Something has to change."

"What's the matter?" Andrea asked, rubbing sleep from her eyes.

"Listen, Andrea," Greg began. "You've always been the one with the ideas for selling my crafts. When you wanted to get my work into shops, I went along with it. When you wanted the business to grow, I never said no. But our life has gotten out of hand. There is too much going on! All I do is work. Every day. Every evening. Most weekends. And I don't spend enough time with the kids. Do you hear me?"

Andrea was wide awake now. "I hear you," she said. "The business seems to have a life of its own. It's running *us* instead of us running it."

"So you feel it, too?" Greg asked.

"Well, of course I do," said Andrea.

"Everything has been just crazy. But what are we going to do?"

"We need to sort it all out," said Greg. "Tomorrow we'll sit down and take a good look at things. I'm sorry I woke you up. Go back to sleep now."

"OK."

Greg slept like a rock that night. His mind had started to clear, and he was already feeling better.

But Andrea didn't sleep at all. She was thinking all night long. When the first crack of light broke through the bedroom window, she was already wide awake. When Greg came out to the kitchen, she was sitting down at the table with pencil and paper.

"The way I see it, we have three choices," Andrea began. "Choice one: We can cut back the craft business. Way back. Make it very much a part-time thing. Choice two: We can go full time. You quit your job and we see what happens. Or, choice three: We can get out of the craft business completely."

"I don't want to get out of it completely," said Greg. "I love making things. I love getting money for what I make. And I love knowing that my work puts a smile on people's faces."

"OK," said Andrea. "You want to stay in it. The question is—a little or a lot? Part time or full time?"

"That's the question, isn't it?" said Greg. "Here we are with two little kids. Is it a good idea to quit my job? To have no paycheck? It would cost a lot to pay for a health plan. It would be awful to worry about where our next dollar is coming from. Could we make it without a full-time job?"

"What do you think?" said Andrea.

"I want to see some numbers," said Greg. "Which craft shows are really worth doing? Which shops are worth putting my work in? And which of my crafts are selling best?"

"That's what I've been working on,"

said Andrea, looking at her figures.

"Let's look at what you have there," said Greg. "Maybe it will help us decide what to do."

CHAPTER 10

Stepping Out

Andrea and Greg looked at the numbers for quite a while. They saw details they had missed before. Soon the business picture became clearer to them.

Two of the gift shops weren't selling enough. That was an easy decision. Andrea would pull Greg's crafts out of those shops and not ship any more.

Three of the shows were making little more than the rent for the booth. One was even a juried show. When the new contracts for those shows came, Greg would not sign them.

Andrea showed Greg numbers on how well the home workers were doing. One of them wasn't working fast enough. From now on they would pay the workers by the piece instead of by the hour.

Most of the home parties were doing pretty well. But Andrea was doing them alone. She felt that putting on these parties was making her life crazy. Now she decided to continue them only if Greg quit his job.

They could see that being part of the buying co-op was a good deal. No craft store could sell materials for less. Still, there were meetings to attend. And someone always had to go to the co-op to pick up the materials. Andrea found a mail-order book with good prices. Materials by mail would cost a little more. But buying would take much less time. They decided to drop out of the craftworkers' co-op.

Andrea and Greg also looked ahead. If Greg quit his job, how much more could the craft business grow?

They worked out more numbers. They could add a few shows. They could add a few home workers. Best of all, Greg could spend more time on designing his crafts. He could come up with new ideas. He could make bigger and better things.

"So that's the picture," said Andrea. "Now what's it going to be? Will we do crafts full time or cut back a lot?"

They didn't decide that day. Or the next. But on Friday night when Greg came home from work, his mind was made up about one thing.

"Pack a change of clothes," he said to Andrea. "I'll pack some food. We're taking off this weekend."

Andrea threw baby things into a bag. She grabbed some clothes for everyone. Greg packed food in a cooler and tied the tent to the car roof. They put Emma and

Devin in their car seats. Then Andrea got in the car and Greg started driving.

"Do you want to tell me where we're going?" she asked as they headed out past the city limits.

"Remember that camping trip we took a long time ago?" Greg asked. "That was before we were married and had kids and this crazy life. This weekend we're going back to the woods where it all started."

It was almost dark when they got there. By the time the tent was up, the only light came from the moon. Greg built a fire. He stuck hotdogs on a long stick and cooked them over the flames.

"What I really want is to quit my job and do crafts full time," Greg said. "I know it's a little risky. I know it won't be easy. But we're young and life is short. I don't want to live the rest of my days wishing I had done this."

Andrea threw her arms around her husband's neck. "I'm with you," she cried. "All the way!"

On Monday morning Greg gave two weeks' notice at the phone company. His boss said he could stay on the health plan if he paid for it himself.

On Greg's last day at work, his friends gave him a party. He gave each of them a feather pin as a good-bye gift.

The next Monday was the first day Greg didn't have to go to a job. He tried to sleep in. But, as usual, baby Devin got everyone up early.

Greg had two cups of coffee that morning. Then he went into the craft room and got to work. It was a strange feeling, having a whole day ahead to work on crafts. But the hours flew by. The days that followed filled up fast, too. It was as if he had never had a full-time job at all.

Six months later Greg and Andrea sat down and looked at the numbers again. They were good. Greg was making new kinds of jewelry. They had added three shows. They had done their first trade show. And they'd made all the other changes they'd talked about, too.

That's when Greg said, "Let's move. We need a bigger place. Let's look for a house with three bedrooms and a basement for a workshop."

"And lots of wall space," said Andrea. "We'll hang your work like art. Because that's what it is—*art*."

"And then we'll get back to work," said Greg. "Because it's going to take a lot of art to make this work!"

And that it did.